MY STORY MY SOUTH

A Collection of Stories by

DANIEL METTS

MARIGOLD PRESS BOOKS

Published in Savannah, Georgia by Marigold Press Books.

Marigold Press Books titles may be purchased in bulk for educational, business, fundraising, or sales promotional use. For information, please email marigoldpressbooks@gmail.com

Fonts and stock images licensed for commercial use.

Author: Metts, Daniel
Title: My Story My South: A Collection of Stories by Daniel Metts
ISBN: 979-8-9985495-0-2
Library of Congress Control Number: 2025908269
Cover Design: Jodi Caggige
Book Design: Russ Davis, Bravo Book Design

CONTENTS

A NOTE FROM THE AUTHOR

This book started as an "oral tradition" when my children were little. Sometimes, I told them the stories about an experience that one of my parents went through while growing up in the South. In the same way that I listened intently during my parent's recall of a personal event, my children would sit, riveted by my every word until the story was over. Afterwards, they always asked me more questions that I could not answer at the time.

As they grew older, the children, as well as my wife, asked me to write the stories down. One semester, when my wife was teaching an online writing class at a local college, she requested three or four essay-length stories to use in that class. The students' assignment included reading the essays, commenting on them, and finally, interviewing me by video. When the memories of my early life stood out clearly in my mind, I would just sit and go over the event in my thoughts, asking myself, *"Why would God allow that event to happen?"* After a stressful week, it proved to be a kind of therapy for me. Thinking about my family's constant requests to write down the oral stories, I decided to write them on my own. Finally, within the last four months, my wife asked me to write more and compile them into a book. I had just lived through watching all the effort she put into her book. I told her, "If you serve as my chief editor, I will write it." Now I was committed—and here it is!

A NOTE FROM ROSE (MARCIA)

After my first ever self-published book, my friends continually asked me, "So where's your second book?" I didn't have a second book. I certainly wasn't going to make a sequel to A Turtle's Tale, that creation from a once-in-a-lifetime event about which I was passionate. Any sequel lacked such "passion," which readers would have spotted right away. However, I could see another book brewing. My husband had already written three stories (and told me countless others), so I requested his authorship of more. After some poking and prodding (mostly for more details), we ended up with sixteen stories! My editorial decisions consisted of maintaining anonymity of individuals and location—I wanted the emphasis to remain on Dan's experiences and the impact they had on his life. The story is arranged mostly in chronological order for the reader's ease, with the exception of two sections that follow their own internal timeline. I've learned so much about my husband during this process; my prayer is that you will also learn, apply, and benefit from the lessons and growth that he experienced.

MY STORY
MY SOUTH

STARTING POINT

My father's family lived in a small town in South Carolina. Born on May 30, 1921, my dad lived in that area until he was about 13 years old. He and my grandfather worked together, doing farm work and any odd job they could find to help feed the family. My grandfather had five children, whom he had been raising alone since my grandmother died when my dad was about 8 years old. Then around 1933, during the Great Depression, it was harder to find work, and the economy became worse for most of the black population.

One day Dad and Grandpa Metts were digging a ditch for a white family, preparing to install a water drain pipe. Dad was bent over digging close to the back porch of the house. The white lady of the house came out onto the back porch, and without looking at who was nearby, emptied a dishpan of dirty water over the side of the porch—right onto Dad's head. His clothes were soaked! Dad lost his temper and reached for a "brickbat" (a small piece of broken brick) to throw at her. The woman screamed and ran into the house.

My grandfather witnessed the incident. Startled at what had happened and afraid of what might happen next, he urged my dad to flee as quickly as possible. He feared the woman's husband might get his gun and gather a few of his friends to beat—or maybe even lynch—my dad.

Grandpa Metts collected his five children that night, and the whole family left South Carolina in a horse-drawn wagon containing all their belongings. After traveling a distance of about 100 miles, probably an eight to twelve hour ride if all went well, they arrived in a small town in North Carolina and lived in the same county for the rest of their lives.

BLACK LIFE

As in most Southern towns, Jim Crow policies colored all of life. Race relations in my hometown were far from perfect, but not as bad as in other parts of the South. We just had to follow the unwritten law that the white men were the superior race.

In school, I remember my teacher would sometimes say things like: "The white man is always going to have things his way." Her words rang true. Black citizens lived in a designated part of town, a substantial distance from downtown or in a gully off the main street. Segregated policies were enforced in the business sector. Black children could enjoy a venture to the movie theater but had to climb the stairs of the fire escape and enter through an outside door that led to the inside balcony. If anyone wanted popcorn or other treats, he or she had to leave the balcony, descend the fire escape, and stand at the back door of the concession stand to order the snack. Restaurants operated the same way; black customers were required to ask for their meal at the back door of the restaurant and take it with them. None were permitted to sit in the restaurant. There was a department store in town with two stories and an escalator that drew the interest of little black children.

A few poor kids and I enjoyed riding the escalator up and down until we were chased off.

Jim Crow laws affected even our verbal interaction with white citizens. From early on, I can remember a certain way my parents would act when talking to white people. They always smiled and spoke in a humble manner during the whole conversation. When my mom received hand-me-down items from them, she often said, "If a white man wants to give you something, go ahead and accept it. You might get something good every now and then." Her advice implied that most times, black folk would be given something the white donors would not use.

Careers were restricted to farm labor or other low-paying jobs, few of them full-time except janitorial positions. Some men worked in the factories; others participated in part-time jobs or day labor. Older boys, like me, did yard work for upper class white families but were paid a pittance. One of our neighbors ran a janitorial business, but black business owners were rare. My grandfather and my dad worked for white folks, laboring in concrete, masonry, and ditch digging, sometimes with a good contract, but usually without one. Dad continued to do such work but had little idea of how to properly charge his customers, mostly out of fear of not getting the job.

Women had fewer opportunities than the men. Black females were consigned to maid work or laundry work for white citizens. My grandmother was the original "pick-up" and "delivery" laundress. She would pick up the customer's clothes and utilize her resources at home: a gigantic black pot—akin to a witch's cauldron—a scrub board, and a metal iron. She boiled water in the pot, inserted the clothing items, and if necessary, removed stains with the scrub board. She hung them on a clothesline to dry, later using an old-fashioned, stove-heated iron to remove the wrinkles. She neatly folded the laundry and returned it to the customer by carrying it in a basket on her head.

My mom often worked as a maid for different white families. One gentleman, a prominent business owner, employed her for his special-needs daughter. As her employer for at least ten years, he exhibited great kindness to Mom, giving her advances when necessary, arranging for Social Security deductions, and even promising to leave something for my mom in his will. After his death, unfortunately, the man's adult children refused to honor his wish, scornfully brushing aside her inquiry.

The careers for blacks with the highest prestige involved the education system. Our schools were segregated for a long time; all the teachers and principals were black. They could afford fine clothes and nice cars; moreover, they enjoyed respect from the common black citizens. One teacher, who taught both my first and second grades, utilized some creative ideas to encourage learning in us youngsters. Unfortunately, all the other teachers, even up to sixth grade, displayed little concern for the students. From first to fourth grade, I rarely ate during school lunchtime, but only one instructor inquired, "You're not going to eat?" When I explained that I had no food at home, she never sought resources for my condition.

For the most part, the teachers were quick to punish seemingly "bad" students. Misbehavior resulted in beatings, especially by the sixth grade teacher. His sole counsel to us boys consisted of a warning as school desegregation appeared on the horizon: "You keep acting like this, and the white teachers know how to take care of you!" The "take-care-of" referred to reform school. My seventh grade teacher warned us about how we were going to be treated differently when the school was integrated. She said that some of us black boys who behaved in a rambunctious manner, even a little bit, would be targeted and possibly sent to reform school.

Reform school[1], a terrible institution, resembled the youth detention centers of today. Anyone sent there had to put on a façade of force to protect themselves from being overcome by another "inmate." Both boys and girls faced the threat of being sent there. My oldest brother, unfortunately, ended up in a reform school. The landlord of the country house we rented owned a farm, and he employed my brother to work on the farm, even teaching him how to drive a tractor. My brother wanted to show off this new skill, so he drove it to our house, a mile from the farm. The landlord's son accused my brother of "stealing the tractor" —a questionable charge considering he had no intention of stealing anything. Yet this charge sent him to reform school. After spending a year at this facility,

---

1 "Reform and Charity Schools," Encyclopedia.com, 2025, https://www.encyclopedia.com/history/news-wires-white-papers-and-books/reform-schools-and-charity-schools

he never seemed the same: always boisterous, a chip on his shoulder, always wanting his own way and constantly getting in trouble.

Eventually, schools were forced to integrate, grade by grade over a period of time. The first year I attended an integrated school was 1969, when I was in eighth grade. To prepare for the influx of white students, the school board removed our black principal and consigned him to an "administration office," keeping him there until he retired. A young white inexperienced principal replaced him. Other black leaders were treated similarly so that none could exercise authority over white students. Some of the white high school students resented the integration and even got in fights, but not all white teens resisted integration. A few white teens joined us black teens in friendly games of pick-up basketball at the town's recreation center. It is amazing how poverty blurs the lines of race. These facets of my hometown had their effect on my family and me. It was in such an environment that I matured from a child to a man.

WATCH AND LEARN

My dad and his family had to do sharecrop work, mainly for food and shelter. Because Dad only made it to third grade, he never learned to read well. To keep in touch with the world, he watched the news on TV. He occasionally told me, "Stay in school, boy. I wish I had." My mom had dropped out of school in ninth grade; however, she could read. In fact, Mom made regular visits to read the Bible to an elderly black lady, who was completely illiterate.

My dad and his dad, Grandpa Metts, had a close relationship. They enjoyed working together, and they would talk and laugh while watching the news or sports, especially wrestling, on the TV at Grandpa's house because we couldn't afford a TV. They also liked attending WWA wrestling matches in person. Dad always showed a lot of respect for his dad, so much so that my mom was a bit jealous of their relationship. Dad and Grandpa Metts were close until he died in 1979 at age 84.

Other than the occasional remark to "stay in school," Dad taught me how to do basic repairs to my shoes so they would last until we could purchase new ones. Sadly, he did not teach me very much at all about how to conduct myself for life. Other than relating the story of his departure from South Carolina, he did not have a close relationship with me. He indirectly taught me a few things; I watched him go to work every day, doing very hard labor. The example of his persistence taught me how to go to work without missing any days.

By her example rather than instruction, Mom taught me how to be humble. In the 1970s, there were a few cases of young black men who were known to associate with white women. One of these fellows was found killed in the rural parts of the county; other similar crimes were never solved. To prevent this from happening to us, Mom taught me and my brothers that white girls were very dangerous to our freedom and safety. When I was a teenager, Mom always warned us not to say anything to a white girl because she considered them "Neck Breakers," meaning they could easily get one of us lynched. Her lesson was one that I never forgot.

Since I had low self-esteem, I did not pursue a girlfriend in high school, but I remember two incidents when my mom's teachings helped me avoid trouble. While I was sitting in my ninth grade Civics class, a white girl, whom I had never met, came to the door and motioned to the teacher that she wanted to talk to me. The teacher called out to me, "Daniel, there is someone at the door who wants to speak with you." When I saw it was a white girl, all I could think about was *Neck Breaker,* so I did not go out to meet her. After class, she was gone, and I was able to relax.

When I was in eleventh grade, I worked a part-time job at a cotton mill. I had just finished collecting rolls of yarn from the spinning machines and placing them into a cart. I pulled the cart to the place for unloading, and a young white girl, who was poor just like me, climbed into the cart as if she wanted my attention. Instantly aware of the danger, I thought *"Neck Breaker!"* I left her and the cart at that spot and rushed away, hoping that no one saw what happened. I was terrified that I might lose my job—or worse.

From watching my parents, I determined that I would deal differently with my own family. I wanted to demonstrate a good example to my growing children and require them to obey my wife and me. I talked with them and encouraged them when they performed well in school and at home. I taught them how to fix things around the house, and I taught my boys how to look another man in the eye, treating that person with respect while requiring the same respect.

ON THE MOVE

Only 10%–20% of black citizens owned their homes; others had to rent. My dad avoided home ownership, mostly because of our low income but also due to a "scam" exacerbated by his illiteracy. One time, my older sister was involved in a car accident, and the other driver was at fault. The insurance agent handling the case asked my dad to sign a paper for the money—which my dad never received. Suspecting that a home purchase involved paperwork, he avoided the issue, settling for a rented place.

Most of the homes we lived in were owned by slum lords, usually renting to low-income residents. We kept moving because if my dad got even a little behind on rent, the owner would tell us to leave. A friend or relative would recommend a place, and our family was on the move again, loading the pick-up truck several times to relocate to the "new" place. Embarrassed about our pitiful possessions, we usually traveled at night. In some ways, it was an adventure for the boys; we explored the surroundings of the new house. The residences I remember are listed below in chronological order.

The "In-Town House #1" (1958–1959) was located on the main drag of the city near the black high school. At that time, our family consisted of six children and my parents. The house had three rooms, running water, and a fireplace for heat. It was built with wood siding and had a dirt yard.

The "Country House" (1959–1960) was about five miles west of the city. It was a sharecropper house of three rooms, with a wood stove for heat. It had no running water, and an outhouse served as our bathroom. We got our water from a hand-operated well pump in the backyard.

The "Duplex House" (1960–1963), close to downtown, sat in a gully near a small river. A few black families lived in this low-lying area, including my maternal grandmother. This place consisted of two duplexes, and we used both sides. Each side had two bedrooms, one bathroom, and a living room/kitchen space. Our family had grown to eleven people by now: two parents and nine children of varying ages.

The "In-Town House #2" (1963–1965) had two bedrooms, one bathroom, a wood stove for heat, and cold running water. My dad started to build a third bedroom but had little knowledge of carpentry. Not only that, the landlord refused to reduce the rent even though he wanted the extra space. The room remained unfinished when we moved.

The "Rural House" (1965–1966), another sharecropper building, was the worst place to live; it was ten miles from town. It had three rooms, a wood stove for heat, an outhouse, and no running water. We had to haul water from the landowner's house on a daily basis after Dad got home from work. From the boys' exploration of the area, we found a natural spring behind the house and used its water for baths, washing, and cleaning the house.

Example of a sharecropper house[2]

The "Big House" (1966–1972), a larger structure, was our longest stay in a residence. A retired school teacher owned it and rented it to our family. A two-story building located in the black section of town, it had cold running water indoors, six rooms, two bathrooms, a fireplace for heat, and a wood stove. We lived in that house until I was 18 years old.

"Public Housing Unit" (1972–1974) was not only our first apartment, it was the first time we ever lived in a place with both hot and cold running water and central heat. I was in heaven! I lived there before entering the Army in June 1974.

---

2 Our Cabin at Allenfarm," Tending the Soil, https://texancultures.utsa.edu/cabin/about-our-cabin/

BREAK-FAST

Due to our low income, food supply was usually skimpy. We ate very basic food: oatmeal or grits in the morning and for dinner, cabbage, potatoes, and dried beans. Any meat consisted of chicken parts like backs, necks, gizzards, livers and hearts—the cheapest parts that could be bought, though some stores just discarded them altogether. One of the scariest times of food insecurity occurred when I was five years old, and we resided in the Country House.

My father, who was a World War II veteran, had gotten very sick and was so weak he could not work. Our food supply was getting low; it seemed like Mom was hardly giving us anything to eat. Dad got so sick that we thought he might die, and we had no medical insurance. A friend with a car brought Grandpa Metts to our house, then took him and Dad to the closest Veterans hospital, which was about 100 miles away. We missed him as soon as the car drove away. My mom was worried; I could see something in her eyes, though I couldn't define it. In a day or two, Grandpa sent word to Mom that Dad had a serious case of pneumonia.

We waited at home. The house was quiet, and the amount of food for nine children grew smaller each day. I remember being hungry and asking Mom for some food one night, just before she put the smallest children to bed. "Wait until morning. Then I can give you something."

I went to bed, eyes wet with tears and rumbling in my stomach.

As the days passed, hunger gnawed at our stomachs, for the food was almost gone. One morning, Mom drew on her long black overcoat. She instructed my oldest sister and brother to keep us in the house until she returned. Her goal was to hike five miles to Grandpa's house and request his assistance in getting food for the family.

We watched as Mom walked down the snow-covered road until she disappeared from sight. Then we were all quiet for a long time—maybe six to eight hours—wondering when she would return. Finally, in the distance, we saw a small black speck on the white snow, coming up the road. As the speck grew larger, we recognized it as Mom. We all hoped that she brought food with her for our hungry stomachs. Even though we celebrated her return, we still wanted to eat. Crestfallen, we saw that her arms held one small bag.

However, hope returned when Mom informed us that Grandpa Metts was not far behind her with more food. Not long after that, we saw a man pushing a wheelbarrow full of bags in the snow-covered road. It was Grandpa!

While we reveled in having both food and Mom back with us, Grandpa told us about their arduous journey.

After Mom had reached Grandpa's house, they rode a cab to the grocery store and purchased the food. But since the snow was so deep, the cab driver declined to drive the fourth of a mile up to our house from the main road. Grandpa told Mom to walk up to the house with one of the food bags while he took the cab back to town to get a wheelbarrow for the rest. After securing the wheelbarrow, the driver took Grandpa back to the place where Mom had been dropped off. He unloaded the remaining bags of food onto the wheelbarrow and pushed it to our house.

A few days later, we received word that my dad was recovered enough to be released from the Veterans hospital. He was coming home! We all rejoiced at the food in our stomachs and the good news of Dad's return.

FROZEN WITH FEAR

Around 1961, when I was 6 years old, my dad owned a pick-up truck. At that time, we lived about two miles from my grandfather's house. One day, Dad let me and one of my older brothers get in the back of the truck and ride with him to Grandpa Metts' house. Since I was the smallest, I got all the way up against the cab of the truck and sat on the floor of the truck bed.

When we arrived, I remained on the truck, sitting in my safe place while Grandpa got in the front seat with Dad and three of my cousins, all older and larger than I, climbed into the truck bed. They all began to horseplay, and I sat tight in my spot on the truck bed, right up against the cab. We had not gone far down the road when one of the boys seated himself near the rear edge of the truck bed, even though the tail gate was down.

All of a sudden, the boys began to scream and holler! My cousin was falling backwards off the truck as we went down the road. Two of the boys were holding my cousin by the hand and trying to keep him from falling all the way off the truck.

Finally, Dad stopped the truck. When the boys pulled my cousin up, I saw blood streaming from his head because it had been striking the paved road up to that point. I was so terrified that I could not move my body at all. The whole scene felt like a slow-motion movie. Dad hopped out of the truck, tied a bandage of some sort to the wound, and headed for the hospital, which was less than a mile away.

I still could not move.

When everyone entered the hospital, I sat alone in the truck. It started to get dark and cold, and I still could not move or speak. I felt frozen in that spot on the truck bed. As time went by, I began to move my head and my hands a little, slowly coming back to myself. I remember wondering, *"When will everybody come out of the hospital?"*

After a long while, I heard familiar voices coming back to the truck. Some of the boys were told to walk back to Grandpa's house. I looked into the back window and saw my injured cousin sitting on the truck seat with bandages on his head. Although I was relieved to see him, I still felt unable to call out to anyone in the truck.

When we got back to Grandpa's house, everyone else exited the truck and was greeted by those in the house. No one was crying or yelling anymore, but I still could not move my body. Then I heard someone call my name: "Where is Daniel?"

I still could not move.

My mother fretfully called my name again. Her voice seemed to give me the strength to move my body and speak. I stood up in the truck bed and said, "Here I am, Mama."

Helping me out of the truck, she was happy, and I was warm again. Everybody realized I had curled myself up so tightly that I could not be seen in the truck bed. They all began to laugh at how I hid so well, and I laughed too. Many years later when I was in the military, I realized that I had been in shock, frozen with fear; that's why I couldn't move.

FOWL TALES

When we lived in the "Big House," my dad got the bright idea to raise chickens. He ordered one hundred tiny "peeps" for five dollars from a local hatchery. He brought the 3-day-old chicks home in a cardboard box. Since Dad was a construction worker, not a farmer, he put the baby chicks on our back porch and told us to look after them while he was at work. Well, my younger brothers and I had no idea what to do for baby chickens. We tried to give them water and bread crumbs, but it was in the late fall. When it got cold at night, the chicks would huddle together, but they just could not keep warm. Within about a week, they all died. We simply had no idea of their sensitivity to cold weather.

When I was about 7 years old, we siblings always liked to go to my maternal grandmother's house because she always made fried chicken, potato salad, biscuits, and cake. She gave us as much as we wanted to eat, and we loved her for it. She always raised her own chickens, and we kids used to chase them around her yard until she made us stop. But we never made the connection between the chickens we chased and the chickens we ate at her table.

Much later, when I was about 12 years old, I visited my grandmother just at the time when she was preparing to kill chickens and replenish her freezer. She made a fire around her gigantic wash pot, the one that looked like a witch's cauldron, and filled it with water. She caught one chicken, wrung its neck, stepped on its head with her foot, and pulled the chicken's feet until the head popped off. Then she threw it down to let it flop around and bleed out. She proceeded with the same treatment to another chicken. I viewed the whole process as pretty gruesome. However, after a few kills, she told me to get a chicken and kill it. I hesitated, but I knew better than to disobey her, so I caught a chicken, but instead of stepping on its head, I laid it on the chopping block, took her axe, and chopped the chicken's head off.

After they all bled out, she showed me how dipping them in the boiling wash pot helped the feathers come off more easily. After we plucked them all, she gutted them, and we washed the bodies off with a water hose. Later, she packed them in her freezer. I finally made the connection between the fried chicken we ate at her table and how they got there.

When I was about 14 years old, my mom worked as a house maid for some white families in town. One of the families she cleaned for had an old rooster that kept waking them up every morning. They had endured enough of its noise, so they asked Mom if she wanted a rooster. In those days, a maid never refused a gift from the family she worked for. Mom brought the rooster home to the "Big House." Since we lived in town, there was no chicken pen outside, so we put him in our basement. The rooster woke us up every day with its crowing, a sound that reached every room in the house. But we became used to his presence, treating him almost like a pet.

After one month, Mom noticed that our family had run out of meat, with no money to buy any more. She made the sorrowful request for me to catch the bird and kill it so that she could make chicken and dumplings. While a bit sad myself, I was also ready for some meat.

Having the training from my grandmother, I knew exactly what to do. I took the rooster from the basement, went outside, and killed him quickly. I performed every step my grandmother had taught me and brought the finished product to Mom. She proceeded to cook it in a pot with the dumplings. We all ate the delicious meal quietly, and satisfying our hunger overcame the sadness of losing our pet. Mom finally expressed the thoughts in our minds: "Well, we will miss the old rooster."

BIDDING WAR

When I was about 12 years old, my father told me about an old lady for whom he had just finished some construction. He said to me, "Boy, you know how to cut grass?"

I replied, "Yes."

He said, "Go downtown to Mrs. Jones' house on Cider street. She's a widow woman and wants a boy to mow her grass. She will pay you fifty cents an hour." He smiled as he walked away.

I was glad for a chance to make some money; now I could buy candy on my own! Off I went to Mrs. Jones' house. She showed me how to start the mower and where to cut; she also showed me what not to cut, namely her flowers. I worked for her two hours each Saturday, and she paid me one dollar each time. If I did a good job, she would give me an extra quarter for a tip.

I considered myself a good worker because one day after I finished working in her yard, she said to me, "I told a member at my church about you, and she wanted to know if you could come and cut her grass after you finish cutting mine." When I agreed to this extra job, she gave me the address of Mrs. Stilbrook, her church friend, but she also expressed a concern. "I am afraid she might try to take you away from me because her husband is a dentist, and they can pay you more than I can."

I went to the house of the dentist's wife, Mrs. Stilbrook, who also explained how she wanted her grass to be cut and what not to cut. After I was finished, she announced, "I am going to pay you one dollar per hour to work for me because fifty cents an hour is not enough." Realizing where I could make the most money, I ceased working for Mrs. Jones.

One day after I finished cutting her grass, Mrs. Stilbrook told me that Mrs. Jones wouldn't speak to her anymore. "I think she is angry with me because she thinks I stole you away from her." Her remark came with a sly Southern smile. I felt a little guilty about letting Mrs. Jones down. I decided to relieve my guilt by sending my younger brother to her house to work in her yard for fifty cents per hour.

PHOTOS

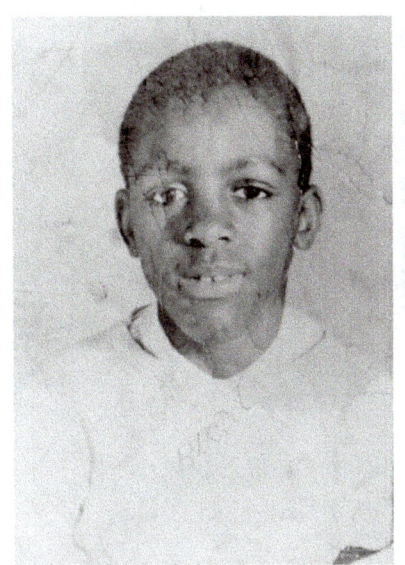

School Picture 1963

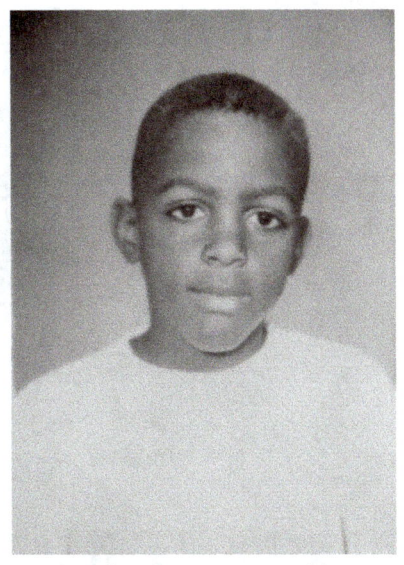

School Picture 1964

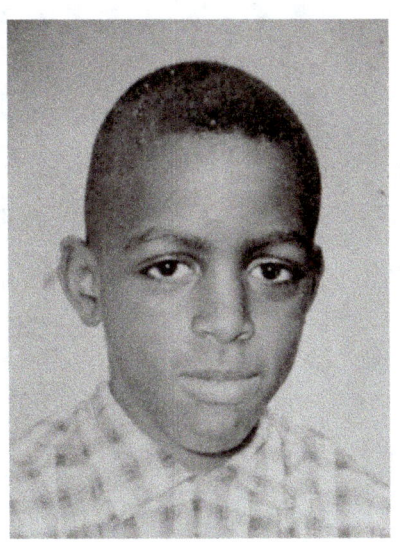

School Picture 1965

Boot Camp Sharpshooter

Boot Camp Exercise

Boot Camp Fellow Comrades

Boot Camp Graduation

Prep for Parade at Ft Campbell

Official Photo Ft Meade

Fishing at Ft Meade

Dan in Barracks Ft Meade 1979

Prep for photo job

Photo job

Gremlin at Ft Meade

Marcia and Son

Reading the Bible 1979

Wedding Day

A&P school in NC

BLACK, WHITE, & BLUE

The police officers in my town were not friendly to the black male population. The white policemen always treated young blacks badly, but the black officers were even worse. With the Civil Rights movement going on, the city fathers wanted to keep things quiet in the black section of town, so they hired their first two black police officers—two old black guys already past retirement age— to mainly patrol the black section. One of the token black officers killed one black suspect who resisted arrest. As a result, they were not well liked in the black community.

I had encounters with both white and black officers on different occasions. When I was 18 years old, two white policemen picked me up as a suspect for breaking into a store near our housing project. They even attempted to get a confession for my alleged break-in. At some point during the interrogation, one policeman said he had a witness who spotted me coming out of the store. I asked him, "Where is your witness?" Surprisingly, he let me go. If I had given in, I would have had an arrest record.

The black officers played a more dangerous game. One day in 1969, when I was 14, I experienced their duplicity firsthand as I was leaving my part-time job. I had been working for Dr. Rondoff, a local white dentist, who was formerly a dental surgeon in the Army during World War I. He hired me for yard work: cutting the grass, trimming the hedges, raking leaves—and even non-yard stuff, like cleaning out his garage. After finishing the assigned tasks for that day, I started walking home.

As I meandered down the sidewalk of Main Street, the two black policemen pulled up beside me and asked, "Where are you coming from?"

I replied, "I'm coming from work."

"Where?"

"At Dr. Rondoff's house."

Then they asked, "Have you seen any strange black guys around here?"

I thought for a moment, and then replied, "No, not that I recall."

One of them said, "Well, this white girl claims that some black guy raped her. How about taking a ride with us? We'll go to her house and let her look you over—to see if you're the one who did it."

Shrugging my shoulders, I naively entered the police vehicle. I hadn't done anything, so what did I have to fear?

The house was in a very upscale section of town about two blocks from the dentist's house where I had been working. After arriving at the girl's house, the men knocked on the door, and the girl and her mother came out and stood on the porch.

I sat in the patrol car, completely clueless. The seriousness of my situation had not dawned on me yet.

The black officers asked me to get out of the car and stand facing the girl and her mother. One officer pointed to me, his lips moving, and I knew what he was asking her.

Then the girl shook her head, indicating the word "No."

The officers asked me to get back in the car and drove me back to the same spot on Main Street where they picked me up. On the way, they asked again if I had seen any strange black boys in town that day.

My answer was still, "No."

What if the girl had nodded her head the other way? Would I have suffered the fate of a less fortunate black teenager, far from my town? Emmett Till—his name was whispered among older black citizens in my town after 1955. I was not aware of him until much later, when our black teacher in the segregated junior high school mentioned the incident. Before his visit to Mississippi, Emmit's mother "warned him that Southern whites… could react violently to behaviour that was tolerated in the North."[3] Heedless of her advice, he succumbed to a risk: a peer "dared Till to talk to the store's cashier, Carolyn Bryant, a white woman." The drastic reaction to an accusation and the horrible incident of his death followed shortly thereafter.

But this incident was far from my mind. Even as I walked the rest of the way home, I still did not understand

---

3 Michael Ray, "Emmett Till: American Murder Victim," Britannica, 2025, https://www.britannica.com/biography/Emmett-Till

the seriousness of the situation in which those black officers had put me. Not until years later, when I was serving in the U.S. Army, did I realize how my life was in danger. When I think back on that time now, I see that God preserved my freedom, and I thank Him for it.

THE BOY WHO TOOK THINGS APART

One activity that really boosted my confidence while growing up was dismantling and reassembling things. I always had a curiosity about how mechanical things worked. It started with mere observation, and then I began venturing into my own experiments, some which got me into trouble. These incidents occurred at different stages in my life, and even though I did not know the meaning of the word "curiosity," I know now that's what I felt each time.

At the Country House

When I was about 4 years old, we had no running water in the house, so we had to use a hand-operated pump in the backyard that drew water from a well. Whenever my dad worked the handle, I watched the pump intently. When the water gushed out, I always wondered how the water got from the well to the pump spout. One day, the pump broke, and I finally got that information. Transfixed, I watched as the man who came to repair the pump took it apart.

Then around 5 years old, I noticed a piece of furniture, which regularly caught my attention, the folding metal cot used at night for my brother and me. Whenever we rose in the morning, I watched our mother fold the cot every time. I really wanted to try folding it myself. One morning when my mom left the room, I attempted to fold the cot, ignorant of how to do it safely.

At the time, my 2 year-old brother was nearby, his hand holding onto the cot. As I started to fold, he started screeching. Stunned, I looked over and realized his finger, nearly cut off, was hanging by the skin! As soon as my parents heard his scream, they rushed into the room while I was frozen to the spot. They freed his finger from the cot and whisked him off to the hospital. Thankfully, they got there in time for the doctor to save his finger. I received a spanking and never folded that cot again.

At the Duplex House

When I was about 7 years old, we had an old Kerosene cook stove that fascinated me. I would watch intently as my mother lit the wicks for the burners. When she put fuel oil in the storage tank, I tried to figure out how the oil flowed from the tank to the burner wick. She had to turn the tank upside down to attach it back to the stove, and I noticed that the screw-on cap for the tank had a spring-loaded stem in the middle of the cap. There was a gurgling sound as the fuel oil flowed from the tank into the pipe that supplied the burners with oil. Time after time, I watched her light that stove. When I started fiddling with the buttons, she would slap my hand, "Boy, don't touch that!" This warning occurred at least three times.

One time when Mom was in the house but not nearby, I tried to light the stove by myself. The oil was already in the tank, so all I had to do was to light the burner. However, there were too many fumes from the fuel build-up, and when I struck the match, the stove ignited rapidly with a loud POOF! The flames shot out and burned my eyelashes. My mom rushed into the kitchen. She made sure I was all right and then scolded me, "Boy, what you tryin' to do! You mighta set the house on fire!" I got a good spanking, and I never tried it again.

When I was 8, a stray kitten wandered into our yard, which I played with outside. A wood burning stove sat outside the house, and a pile of wood blocks lay nearby. I decided to build a house for the kitten with the wood blocks. I stacked them to make a square-shaped space large enough to fit the kitten's size, and I put the kitten in the space. I selected more blocks wide and long enough to form a roof, and I made sure to create a doorway for the kitten to get out. I was so proud of building this house for my new kitten friend. I talked to the kitten through the doorway opening and imagined that the kitten was talking to me with its meows.

Suddenly, my 13-year-old brother stepped from the doorway of our duplex onto the little house, causing it to collapse and instantly kill the kitten. My brother just laughed and walked away. Seeing its blood on the wooden blocks, I ran to my mom. My mother disapproved of my brother's behavior, but nothing more was ever done. We discarded the kitten in the woods, and I was in shock for a while. Though I disliked my brother after that, I never took any action because I was afraid of him. After all, his temperament had changed for the worse after reform school, and I decided to avoid any backlash from a verbal protest.

At In-Town House #2

When I was 9 years old, I wondered about the masonry tools on the back of my dad's old pick-up truck. I asked Dad about the hammer, trowel, builder's level, folding ruler, and hand saw, wondering what each was used for. Sometimes when my dad was not looking, I would borrow one or more of the tools and pretend to be building something.

Once, I borrowed his hammer, found a piece of wooden board and some nails, and went to work. I nailed the board to the side of the house so it extended from the side of the house like a shelf. I then found another board and attached it like a leg to a table. I gently stepped up onto the little shelf to see if it could hold my weight. When it did, I was very proud of myself and proceeded to tell my parents. Mom congratulated me on a good job, but Dad scolded me and tore it down. He reminded me that the house was rented, not owned. I failed to understand that homeowners didn't like renovation to their property without permission; I only felt that my dad's criticism seemed like a lack of support, which saddened me.

At the Big House

When I was 13, Dad brought home an old kitchen stove and left it outside in our junk pile. I wanted to tinker with it and take it apart, but I didn't have any tools. However, I did have an old pocket knife, which I used to remove some screws in the stove. The knife suddenly closed on my index finger and sliced it to the bone!

I pulled the knife apart to get it off my finger, then I wrapped a piece of cloth around it. I went up the road to my grandparents' house, dripping as my blood soaked the cloth.

My aunt exclaimed, "Hol' that thing on there and git in the car!" She immediately drove me to the hospital.

Thankfully, our family doctor was in the emergency room. He eyed me suspiciously. "How did this happen? You been in a fight?"

I explained my experiment with the pocket knife and the old stove.

Still looking squint-eyed, he washed it off, put stitches in the finger, and bandaged it up. Knowing our poor financial situation, he never asked for money, not even this time.

When I got home, I explained my wound to my parents. My dad warned me, "Boy, don't you mess with that stove with no knife!" A few days later—despite his warning—I fiddled with the stove again, but this time with a butter knife.

THE KNIFE

Growing up, public schools were segregated, and the black school I attended contained all the grades from first to twelfth in a building with two wings. Mr. Sydney, our black principal, had been at that school since 1952. A tall, dignified man, he had seen and experienced the trials of being black much more than I had in my young life.

When I was 14 years old, we had our first year of racial integration at my school, which included only eighth to twelfth grades. Mr. Sydney was removed from our school, transferred to the county Board of Education office, and given a "do-nothing" job. Mr. Frist, a new, young, white principal who had never been in charge of a school before, replaced Mr. Sydney.

At the time, my homeroom teacher, Mr. Goon, was an older white man who had been a teacher and a football coach for a long time in our county. But it was also his first time teaching at an integrated school.

I was very nervous about how things would go for me with the new rules, especially since I was already lacking in self-confidence. And because my family was very poor, I could not afford to dress like most of the white kids.

Sure enough, trouble found its way to me.

A small group of white classmates started harassing me, urging me to fight Jerry, a stout white boy whom they thought could beat me. I could tell Jerry did not want to fight anymore than I did, but the instigators kept at it. They wanted to see us fight!

I didn't have any weapons except an old, discarded pocket knife. One day before school, I was sharpening the pocket knife on a stepping stone in our front yard. When it was time to walk to school, I closed the knife and put it into my pocket. In the back of my mind, I knew not to bring the knife to school, but I took it anyway.

During morning recess, three boys came towards me in a dimly lit part of the hallway and corralled me into a corner, still trying to get me to fight Jerry. The instigators chanted to Jerry: "Get him boy! Get him!" Meanwhile, they had backed me into a corner, blocking my exit. Before I realized it, Jerry pushed me and snarled, "Let's fight!" Without thinking, I reached in my pocket for the knife, unfolded it, and swiped at Jerry's neck, not intending to cut him badly but enough to get him to back off. It was a gentle swipe, but I spotted a trickle of blood on his neck, similar to a cut from shaving with a safety razor.

I panicked. So did the three boys who ran off, two of them yelling, "Daniel cut Jerry!"

Despite my panic, I closed the knife, put it back into my pocket, and walked to the front of the school hallway. I was met by Mr. Goon, who asked me to give him the knife. I handed it to him without a word and walked with him to the school office. Mr. Goon had already seen that

Jerry's cut had barely broken the skin—only enough to bleed, but not even serious enough to see a doctor.

Mr. Goon took me into the school office to Mr. Frist, the school principal. After hearing about the incident, Mr. Frist panicked. This young principal probably was only thinking about his job security—not about me, Jerry, or the instigators. Noting Mr. Frist's timidity, Mr. Goon took charge of the situation and immediately accused me. "You were going for his jugular vein, weren't you?"

I replied, "Don't I have the right to defend myself from these boys who were ganging up on me?"

Mr. Goon slapped my face heavily with his hand. Anger rose up inside of me, but I resisted the urge to fight him; instead, I ran out of the office, out of the school, and all the way home. I told my mom all that happened and then started to cry. Mom reassured me, speaking in a comforting tone. She assured me all would work out "by the help of the Lord"—a saying she used when she was not sure what to do next. (When I think about that statement now, she was uttering a prayer of sorts.) Her tone began to comfort me, and I stopped crying. We sat there in silence for a while. But I also realized there was going to be trouble: a black boy who cut the white boy the first week—right after the school was integrated! People who doubted that integration would work might point at me and say, "See!?"

About that time, my Dad came home from work to get some materials necessary for his job. My mom told him about the incident. Dad looked at me and said, "Boy, what did you do?"

I replied, "I didn't do anything to start this mess."

Impatient with my answer, he snarled, "Boy, you know you did something!"

Hearing his comments, both condemning and judgmental, I started crying again, and even Mom's eyes were tearful as she chastised Dad for his lack of care about the seriousness of the situation. Dad turned around, walked back to his truck, and drove away. I was hurt and disappointed that he didn't seem to understand my feelings or offer a helpful solution.

About thirty minutes passed while Mom and I just sat there. She was trying to figure out the next best thing to do. Mom was not an aggressive person, but she would always do her best to help her children no matter the situation.

Unbeknownst to me, one of the black teachers had called Mr. Sydney, our former principal, and told him about the incident. So it was to my surprise that a car pulled up at our house that same day. Out stepped Mr. Sydney.

He walked up, greeted us and said, "Okay, young man; tell me your side of the story."

I told him everything that happened. Examining my face, he could see where Mr. Goon had struck me. He said, "I want you to go back to school tomorrow; do not worry about anything. That teacher should have never hit you like that. You go on back to school tomorrow; it will be all right." After he returned to his car and drove off, Mom and I breathed a sigh of relief.

The next day I went back to school and to my homeroom teacher, Mr. Goon. He welcomed me back into the classroom, and the class proceeded as if nothing had ever happened.

FINDING MY NICHE

Slowly, I began to see that each time I worked with my hands, I became more skilled. Still not understanding why such activities fulfilled a longing, I proceeded to launch out, attempting to do more things on my own.

At the Big House, when I was 14 years old, an old wringer washing machine sat on the back porch. Someone had to regularly fill a bucket with water from the kitchen sink, carry it to the machine, and pour it in. The machine would swish the clothes back and forth until it was manually turned off. This chore usually fell to my mom, and for anyone, carrying that water to the machine was heavy work. So, I started looking for a way to help Mom.

We had an outdoor faucet on the side of the house near the back porch. I wanted to see if I could connect a hose to the faucet and route it up to the washing machine. When I went to look at the faucet, I noticed that the steel pipe that came up out of the ground was cracked from being frozen over the winter. I unscrewed the damaged section and was determined to get a new section made to replace it.

I went to a plumber's shop and asked him about making the necessary piece. He seemed a little surprised that I was able to remove the cracked section on my own and asked me several questions about my plans to install the new section. Before I left the shop, he gave me a small container of what he called "pipe dope." He explained how to apply some of the "dope" to each end of the new pipe threads before installing to keep the pipe from leaking.

As I walked home, I wondered why the plumber was so helpful. My mom said the plumber must have noticed I had some mechanical ability and would make a good plumber someday. I connected the pipe according to the plumber's directions, and when I turned the water on, the faucet worked well—no leaks! I was proud of my work.

The experience with the plumber provided good feedback. Through my years of growing up, I endured many discouraging comments from extended family and others. However, I made it to high school by God's grace. Since my academics were poor up to that point, I was doubtful about even finishing high school. In fact, I planned on dropping out of school when I turned 16, like my three older brothers had done before me. However, the officials who looked at my academic record selected me for enrollment in vocational track courses. It was through these classes that I really matured in the skill of working with my hands.

Only male students filled these classes, held during the first two hours of the morning. Those in the ninth and tenth grades participated in carpentry only; their space was located in the basement of the main school campus. The eleventh and twelfth grade students worked in both carpentry and bricklaying and took an activity bus to a facility across town for their classes. Their vocational space, about the size of a basketball gymnasium, had block walls, concrete floors, and a roll-up door for each side that enabled access to the particular shop.

My first period class in ninth grade was "Basic Carpentry as a Trade." My carpentry teacher was a pleasant 60-year-old white man, who seemed to care about the students. He began by displaying all the carpentry tools and showing us how to use them safely. We learned how to utilize power tools for cutting wood and how to use an electric sander to create a smooth surface for painting. We also learned how to use the measuring devices to ensure a good product. Listening daily to his loud but reassuring voice, I thought to myself, *"I could do well in this class!"* My mom had once predicted that I would be a carpenter when I grew up. Now I was starting to believe it!

I made my first wooden project in this class, which I still possess today: a gun rack. After measuring a piece of wood for the rack, I traced a pattern onto the wooden piece and utilized the appropriate tools to cut it. I used the band saw to make the curves of the rack where the guns would lie. After nailing it together, I used an electric sander to smooth the surface, then sanded it by hand. The instructor demonstrated how to use a "nail set," a small device placed upon each nail; in that way, I could tap the nail head slightly below the surface of the wood. I filled in the dents with putty, waited until it dried, sanded again, and stained it.

Gun Rack

Telephone Table

I proudly received an "A" on the rack. In fact, I earned an "A" on all my projects in the class. Carpentry class was the first high grade I'd ever received in my school career. It not only boosted my grade point average but also my self-esteem. Armed with this newfound sense of empowerment, I never failed any of my vocational classes.

In twelfth grade, I was determined to make a telephone table with a shelf and single drawer. After surveying various examples of telephone tables provided by the teacher, I decided to build my own from scratch, without a pattern. Today, it sits in the master bedroom—a phone on top, telephone and address books in the shelf section, the drawer cluttered with assorted pieces of paper.

In bricklaying class, we learned about the tools and materials needed for setting up bricks, such as a level and a plumb line, to ensure a valid wall. Our teacher showed us how to mix the mortar to adhere the bricks to one another: permanent mortar with a specific amount of water, sand, and concrete (used for outside jobs) and temporary mortar with a measure of lime and sand. The temporary mortar was used in the classroom so that it could be broken apart. He required the mixture to be performed manually, stirring it in a large metal trough; then, we could use a hand-cranked machine to mix a more instant version of mortar. He also demonstrated how to arrange the bricks to make a wall, patio, or other structure.

Sometimes individuals or businesses in town requested the "free labor" of the vocational students. If the project proved appropriate to our skills (and our practice), the inquirer would purchase all materials for the project, and the class would travel to the site to work. Sometimes our instructor initiated the project by laying the foundation; then we continued to arrange the bricks. We constructed brick projects, such as a wall, a set of stairs, a patio, and a fence. We even created a wall with a lattice pattern to adorn a man's driveway with his leftover bricks. One project—a shed for a local cemetery—involved both brick and carpentry. All of these projects provided real-life practice, which could apply to personal use or paid opportunities later.

I achieved an overall high "A" in all those classes. I was determined to finish high school. I repeated a history class, a requirement for graduation, and graduated in May 1974. As I look back on the success of those high school classes, I see that my penchant for mechanical things and for working with my hands, had finally been realized. Even now, I am so thankful for that vocational track. How sad that such classes, available back then for all teen boys in the area, have been moved to only one specialty school. Who knows how many more of today's teen boys may have been inspired by working with their hands as I did!

BOOT CAMP

After I graduated from high school, I entered U.S. Army boot camp on July 26, 1974. It was my first time living away from home, and I was about to do a lot of growing up really fast.

The first day of boot camp was quite a shock. At the reception station, each man was assigned a duffle bag, a sturdy cloth bag for storing official military clothing and our personal belongings. Then we recruits were loaded onto "cattle cars," eighteen-wheeler metal trucks. Since the trucks had been sitting in the hot July sun for hours, they felt like ovens. The drill sergeants screamed and cursed at us while pushing us into each truck; we were packed in like sardines. Though the ride from the reception station to the assigned company was about three miles, we dripped with sweat upon arrival and met our barrack's platoon sergeant. The sergeant flung open the doors on each "cattle" truck, yelled at each recruit, and cursed us as we exited. Then we were told to stand in a straight line and listen to his instructions.

Certain personal items were not permitted in our duffle bag. To ensure the omission of those items, we were ordered to lift the bags high above our heads and with all our strength, slam them to the pavement several times. Such action would break anything that was forbidden—something that should not have been in the bags in the first place. Then we were told to straddle the bags and, at the sergeant's command, jump up, extend our legs forward, and let our buttocks fall astride the bags so that any sharp edge inside would cause pain upon straddling the bags. Thankfully, I had only soft items in my bag.

Then we were marched up the hill to our barracks and assigned three things: a bunk bed, a small wall locker, and a foot locker. After being shown how to store our things, we were told to expect an inspection the next morning. By the time everything settled down, it was about 5:30 PM. As I went to sleep that night, I wondered to myself, *"What in the world have I gotten myself into?"*

However, I gradually adjusted to life in "Basic Combat Training" (BCT). By my second week of BCT, I was promoted to Private E-2. As the senior drill sergeant pinned the stripe on my uniform in front of the platoon, I felt pride at my accomplishment. Within the next week, he assigned me to the position of squad leader while I was in Charlie Company.

In the Army, one company consists of 160 men and each company consists of four platoons. Each platoon has forty men divided into four squads of ten men. As a squad leader, I exercised basic leadership, including a regular scrutiny of the squad's appearance. Was each man dressed suitably, sporting appropriate haircuts, and wearing freshly shined boots? If any of these elements appeared amiss, my task involved making sure the men were in order at the next inspection.

One incident stood out from the various events of BCT. The entire platoon performed poorly on one of our morning runs of two miles. All along the way, the sergeant yelled and cursed at us, denigrating us as "sorry." After finishing the run, we stood in formation; four lines of ten men, each forming a triangle-shaped group. The sergeant fussed and cursed at us some more and finally shouted, "There will be no more smoke breaks until you all get in better shape!"

He then strolled into the company orderly room. We remained standing outside until told to do otherwise but took this opportunity to catch our breath and rest. I happened to look down the row of my ten-man squadron. To my shock and anger, one man had taken out a cigarette, lit it, and began to smoke.

I lost my temper.

I marched over to the smoker, snarling, "You heard the sergeant just say, 'No more smoking.' Put that cigarette out now!"

The man opened his mouth to protest.

Instinctively, I slapped the cigarette out of his mouth.

Registering shock at first, the guy grew angry. In the squad behind mine, some of his "home boys" also reacted. In fact, one of them unshouldered his M-16 rifle and raised it to strike me.

Suddenly, the sergeant opened the door of the orderly room. All the men in the platoon instantly scrambled back to their position in line. The sergeant observed the activity as he walked by all the men and headed in our direction.

I thought, *"Uh, oh. Now, I'm in trouble."*

Instead, the sergeant, half smirking, called the platoon to attention and gave the command to march. Even after we marched to our next instruction session, he never said a word to me. The man who had brandished his rifle later threatened me: "I'll bust your head open if you hit my friend anymore!" However, some of the men in the platoon thanked me for my impulsive action.

In about the fifth week of BCT, all was going well, and the company was down to the number of those who would actually graduate. About four to six men had been kicked out for a number of reasons, such as disobedience or weak upper-body strength. Everyone else who had passed all the necessary criteria would graduate in three weeks. I realized that I was about to accomplish something great.

By the last week of BCT, October 1974, I was on the parade field at the fort with the rest of the company, await-ing our graduation ceremony, which included "pass in review"—that is, marching past all the visiting dignitaries, mostly high-ranking military officers. I was a happy young man, carrying much more confidence and pride than I had just three months earlier. I was a soldier now.

After receiving orders of where to report for technical training, I took advantage of the ten-day "leave" (vacation) after boot camp. When I returned to my parent's house, I wore my uniform. As they expressed pride at my appearance, I marveled at my accomplishment.

BEHIND THE BLADES

The time arrived to report to my next base for technical training. I wore my military uniform, and my parents drove me to the airport where I caught a flight to Fort Benjamin Harris, Indiana. I remained there for two weeks, waiting for a training class to open at Chennault Air Force Base, Illinois. I finished the required training in late January 1975 and arrived a month later at my permanent duty station—Fort Campbell, Kentucky—where I was assigned as an Army aircraft mechanic for the 101st Airborne Division (Air Assault). I became a part of the 101st Aviation Battalion, Alpha Company, Attack Helicopter Company.

My job training involved three specific types of Army helicopters,[4] which were the backbone of Army aviation at that time. My high school vocational training helped me considerably because it gave me four years of experience developing good hand-eye coordination with various hand tools. My sergeant put me with an experienced mechanic to begin showing me how to work on our aircraft. The

---

4 "A Look at the Top Helicopters of the Vietnam War," Chopperspotter.com, 2022, https://www.chopperspotter.com/a-look-at-the-top-helicopters-of-the-vietnam-war/

mechanic would take me to the aircraft under his care and explain what service or repair he was doing and where to find the step-by-step instructions for completing the assigned job. He emphasized the importance of reading the instructions and asking questions while I watched him and handed him tools.

Within the next few weeks, he allowed me to perform various small tasks of repair and service on the aircraft by myself. My trainer required that I carefully inspect each job upon completion, looking for FOD (foreign object damage)—such as a wrench, nut, or bolt left behind after installing a new part. In a worst-case scenario, FOD can cause an aircraft to crash. After a few more weeks of training, I was allowed to work more independently, though all mechanics still needed the supervision of a specially trained Army Aviation Inspector to review the completed work and sign off on it—confirming that it had passed a safety inspection.

In early April 1975, I returned from my shift at the airfield and went down to the Day Room to watch the evening news. Walter Cronkite was reporting on the fall of Saigon in South Vietnam and the evacuation of the U.S. embassy and helicopters from the embassy rooftop. I was a little surprised by the newsreel on the CBS News network. For the first time since joining the Army, it sank in that I was in the military during the Vietnam War. I began to grasp the serious nature of the 1974 oaths: one for enlistment and the other for active duty after BCT.

The 101st had three infantry brigades and one combat aviation brigade; I was a part of the aviation brigade. All the barracks for the fighting brigades were on the same street in this order: 1st, 2nd, and 3rd Infantry, followed by the 101st Aviation Brigade (Combat Support). This meant that if any of the infantry brigades were deployed to combat, part or all of the Aviation Brigade would also deploy to support them. We in the Aviation Brigade were often referred to as the infantry's "bus drivers." The infantry would be delivered to the battlefield and resupplied by helicopters, so we had to learn to be close to the infantry soldiers as well as repair the aircraft as needed.

All members of the 101st Airborne Division had to stay in a high level of physical fitness. We performed calisthenics and ran two miles five days a week. Most units did their run before going to work, so we would be on the road running at the same time as the infantry units. They always called us names and yelled at us as we ran past each other, but we knew it was all in good fun.

Later, I attended Air Assault School. I learned how to install a lifting rig to various vehicles: jeeps, trucks, artillery pieces. This training required repelling down a four-story high tower using a mountain-climbing rope and mountain-climbing rappel seat. A final task involved climbing a ladder of steel cable and aluminum rungs in order to reach the door of a helicopter hovering a hundred feet from the ground. As I climbed the ladder for the first time, I discovered my fear of heights. Thus, I kept a death grip on each rung but made it to the top, where the crew chief pulled me into the helicopter.

Before we could graduate, each student had to complete a forced march of ten miles in a two and a half hour time-span while carrying a backpack, fully loaded M-15 rifle, and full canteen. We also wore a steel helmet with a helmet liner. During temperate weather, it would have been difficult, but we marched in February, enduring sleet and frigid weather. I thought I was going to die. When we arrived at the finish line, steam rose from our steel helmets. However, all but two soldiers in our group successfully completed the march. This grueling exercise encouraged me all the more, knowing that I could handle other hardships in the future.

A SOLDIER'S SURRENDER

Despite growing up in a small town, I rarely attended a church. After taking our family a few times, my parents just stopped going. My exposure to faith occurred first with an elderly female pastor, Mrs. Gordue, who used to preach about hell. The next involved a well-known evangelist. As a teenager, I became interested in watching the Billy Graham crusades on television. Both were instrumental in my coming to faith in Jesus while I was stationed at the Kentucky Army base.

Around June 1975, we moved into new barracks beside the infantry brigades. Since the move coincided with payday, we had a "payday moving" party in our new barracks. Between 8:30 and 9:00 that evening, we spent the time drinking and/or smoking weed. Suddenly, a voice spoke inside my mind: "Are you happy with this lifestyle?"

I didn't think twice, answering the voice with one word: "No." But I resumed my drinking. Music flowed through the room; I watched while the other guys were playing cards and "talking trash." About ten minutes later, the voice returned: "You know what you need to do."

"Yes," I replied. "Yes, I do."

It seemed as if a video tape of a Billy Graham sermon appeared in my mind's eye. He regularly declared, "If you want to accept God as your Savior, say this prayer: 'God, I have sinned against You. I believe that Your Son died on the cross to pay the price for my sins. Please come into my life and save me.'"

After that mental vision, I made an excuse to the guys, left the party, and went back to my room, not far down the hall. I got down on my knees and prayed: "God come into my life; give my life meaning and purpose. Save me!" Immediately after that prayer, I felt a presence, like somebody was in the room with me. It also felt like a great burden had been lifted off my back.

The Billy Graham tape started playing in my head again: "If you have accepted Jesus as your Savior, read the Bible and go to church." After I rose from the floor and went to bed, I felt like a different person than the one who attended the party. The next day, I visited the Post Exchange, a store on the military base, and purchased a Bible, a "Living New Testament" with illustrations. I read that Bible all day Saturday, stopping only to eat my three meals.

Arising on Sunday morning, I ate breakfast and walked to the closest chapel, one with a Protestant worship service. When the Chaplain started to preach, my brain was like a sponge, soaking up everything in the sermon. After lunch, I returned to my room in the barracks and read the Bible for the rest of that day. I couldn't put the book down! Though not fully comprehending it then, I knew that

God had come into my life, and because I belonged to Him, I was no longer the same person.

Returning to work on Monday, the guys inquired about my whereabouts all weekend. I responded, "I am saved; I'm a Christian." Someone labeled me "Jesus Freak." For the next several months, that was my name at work: "Jesus Freak." No longer drinking beer or wine, I established a new routine for the weekend: reading the bible and attending church. As a result, I grew in faith and in the knowledge of God. I began to talk to guys in the barracks about my life and how God had changed me. Though some rejected me, others were curious.

WARFARE WITHIN

While my life changed, I certainly wasn't perfect. I found that out in a spat with a supervisor. While stationed in Fort Campbell, Kentucky, the 101st was training for a fall 1976 deployment to Germany— Reforger 1976. The massive training event involved many Americans, along with allied units from the United Kingdom and Europe.

One morning after breakfast, I had to meet my new senior sergeant outside the mess hall and ride to a railhead on base. The mission was to train us to load trucks and trailers onto flatbed rail cars and properly secure them for transport. The vehicles would then be shipped to Norfolk, Virginia, where they'd be loaded onto transport ships that were bound for Germany.

That morning, I drank too much coffee at breakfast and was jittery from the caffeine when I met up with my sergeant and two fellow workers. On the way to the railhead, the sergeant got lost—he was new to the base and unfamiliar with the roads. With every wrong turn, I made a smart remark, and by the time we arrived at the railhead, he was clearly upset with me.

We departed the truck, and the civilian supervisor began the training. As each man guided a truck up the ramp onto a flatbed, we helped direct the driver to the designated position. We learned two other important tasks: how to install chocks under the truck's tires and how to tie the wheels to the tie-down pad on the flatbed floor. For stability, we used high-gauge steel wire, twisting it tight to secure the tie-down. As I was following the instructor's directions, the senior sergeant suddenly stopped me and shouted, "You're not following the right procedure!"

My anger rose. Then my sergeant walked up to the flat bed and barked, "Get down! At ease!"

I knew his order of "at ease" actually meant, "*Shut up and let me talk!*"

I obeyed. Then he ripped into me, "I'm tired of your insubordination; I'm going to straighten you out!"

I kept silent for a short while as he fussed, and when he stopped talking, I retorted, "Well, if you are not going to say anything else, I am going to say something. A civilian instructor can't talk to me like he is my sergeant. He can't give me any orders!"

At that point, several of the nearby warrant officers yelled, "Shut up!" One of them, standing closer to me, lowered his lit cigarette and accidently burned me on the arm.

I was about to go berserk!

However, a captain, who had been watching the incident and standing about fifteen feet away, called out in solemn tone: "All of you need to calm down before someone gets into serious trouble."

That broke the tension; all of us calmed down and returned to the training. I climbed onto the flatbed, and the same civilian instructor instructed me to complete the truck tie-down procedure. This time, I kept a cool head until the training was over for that day.

As I rode back to the barracks with my sergeant and the two co-workers, I wondered whether excess caffeine and sugar had been a factor in the conflict. Now, looking back on that event, I realize that while caffeine may have contributed to my insolent speech and helped spark the conflict, the devil was also waiting for the right moment to try and destroy my Army career.

After that conflict, I realized I still had to work with this sergeant. I prayed and asked God to help me do my job to the best of my ability. I also told myself to follow his orders without backtalk or sarcasm. By God's grace, that negative event transformed into a valuable lesson. That sergeant eventually became a great teacher. He noticed a change in my attitude and once he saw that I wasn't going to be a problem, he began teaching me how to manufacture lines and hoses for the aircraft. Soon, other companies in our battalion started coming to our shop for my expertise in repairing or replacing damaged lines. The sergeant even invited me to fish with him one weekend, but I declined to avoid any appearance of fraternization. Nevertheless, I became one of the best workers in his shop section. A few years later, I was promoted to Corporal and then to Sergeant, both at his recommendation. God is good!

The six-week trip to Germany was my first time out of the country, but I didn't do much while I was there. In our "tent city" of about 150 tents, we had a tent for everything. There were housing tents, which were roomy and sturdy, a large mess hall tent for meals, a German cuisine tent that offered beer, bratwurst, cognac, and fried potatoes, and a movie tent for entertainment.

On the weekends, we had the opportunity to take excursions into Germany. I took a tour of one of the towns, but mostly, I spent time reading in my room—something I rarely did in high school. It was during this time that I discovered A. Conan Doyle's *Sherlock Holmes*. While the pilots flew to their missions, we mechanics stayed in the tent city. Our tasks involved checking the aircrafts before takeoff and upon their return. For the most part, the flights went smoothly—and so did my attitude; there were no more conflicts.

FROM THE PEW TO "I DO"

In 1977, after completing my three-year enlistment in the Army at Fort Campbell, Kentucky, I decided to re-enlist for another three years. I left Fort Campbell in January 1978 and headed to motion picture photography school to retrain for my new job. I graduated from the technical school in April 1978 and was assigned to Fort Meade, Maryland. By this time, I had been a Christian for nearly three years. I missed my chapel family at Fort Campbell, so I started attending chapel worship services at Fort Meade. Upon learning that I had participated in a gospel choir at Fort Campbell, the choir director at the main chapel of Fort Meade convinced me to join the adult choir.

As I settled into on-the-job training (OJT) in my new field, I learned so quickly that my boss began sending me on photo assignments at various units on the base. While I was at work or attending church services, I was happy, and life was good. My outside hobbies included playing pick-up basketball and fishing whenever I could. I also spent time studying the Bible and participating in "The Navigators," a Bible study program for military members. However, there were still some lonely times when I wasn't busy. I had started praying that God would bring a girl into my life who would become my wife. Perhaps I would feel more complete with a wife, for "he who finds a wife finds a good thing and obtains favor from the Lord" (Proverbs 18:22 NKJV).

In June 1979, while singing in the choir at chapel, I noticed a pretty girl sitting in the pews. She stood out from all the other ladies, and I found myself noticing her week after week during the church services. One Sunday, a friend of mine visited and sat in the same pew as her. I later learned they had spoken briefly, and he mentioned that he was visiting to see his friend sing in the choir. After the service, I timed my walk down from the choir risers to coincide with the moment when the choir members would merge with the worshipers filing out of the pews. We all headed to the fellowship hall for coffee, donuts, and punch. Since I ended up right beside her, I struck up a conversation, and we made small talk on the way to the hall. Week after week, these brief encounters allowed us to get to know each other.

Her name was Marcia. She was an Army widow with one young child, living with her parents after the death of her husband. Marcia's father was a U.S. Air Force officer who had served honorably during the Korean and Vietnam wars. I shared with my fellow workers in the photography lab about her. One lady cautioned me to let Marcia know of my interest. At that time, I only knew her name, but I thought I had plenty of time to learn more about her.

Then, one day, I was suddenly sent out of town on

temporary duty (TDY) to Fort Indiantown Gap in Pennsylvania, where I was assigned to provide photography coverage for the National Guard's annual training. The words of the female co-worker echoed in my mind—*What if she finds someone else attractive?* I didn't know her last name, her phone number, or even her address. I had failed to gather any of this information during our chats in the fellowship hall at the Fort Meade chapel. My only recourse was to write to the chapel and hope that she received the message. I purchased a postcard, wrote a message about my whereabouts, and addressed it simply to "Marcia, the Sunday school teacher."

The card arrived at the chapel, and Marcia happened to be at the Sunday school pot-luck supper when the Director of Christian Education handed it to her. He suggested it was probably from one of her Sunday school students. However, when he passed by her a few minutes later, he mentioned that a card had also gone to the choir director! That's when Marcia realized I had sent it.

Marcia wrote back, explaining that she would be out of town for the next few months to finish her graduate degree in Kansas. I really wanted to stay in contact while she was away. So, the next Sunday, Memorial Day weekend, I drove to Fort Meade, hoping to sit with Marcia in the pews during the worship service. When I arrived, we sat together and worshiped. I thought to myself, *"God, this might be the one."*

After the service, I walked back to the fellowship room, intending to ask her if we could keep in touch while she was in Kansas. She spoke with her family and some other friends, while I chatted with a few friends as well. I didn't want to seem like I was only interested in talking to her, but I also didn't want her to leave without asking about writing to each other.

Just as I made my way over to where Marcia was standing, the choir director grabbed me by the arm and started talking. As I listened to her, I noticed Marcia beginning to walk toward me at the same time. I stood there, unsure of how to break away, when Marcia stepped up beside the choir director and said,

"Dan, I am leaving, I will see you later."

I quickly blurted out, "Are you going to write me?"

At that, the choir director realized that Marcia and I wanted to talk, so she made a hasty retreat. I was free! Marcia gave her address to me so that we could stay in touch while she was away.

I returned to Fort Indiantown Gap, and shortly afterward, Marcia and her son flew to Kansas. I was beginning to think about her every day. Marcia spent most of the summer in Kansas finishing her master's degree while I remained on TDY at Fort Indiantown Gap. During that time, we exchanged several letters. After we both returned to Fort Meade and resumed attending church together, we began to date. Six months later, we were engaged, and within a year, we were married at the main chapel on Fort Meade. I realized that I had finally been united with my life partner—I felt more complete as a person.

I separated from the Army after six years of active duty.

Three years after that, we moved to Savannah, Georgia. Marcia began teaching at the college level, I worked at Gulfstream Aerospace for thirty years, and together we raised three children. God has preserved our marriage for forty-five years, and my life and career has been more successful than I ever imagined. We thank God for it all—without Him, nothing this good would have happened to us. Marcia and I hope to continue having a positive impact in the lives of others for as long as we are well enough to do so.